SCIENCE FACTORY

LIGHT & SIGHT

JON RICHARDS

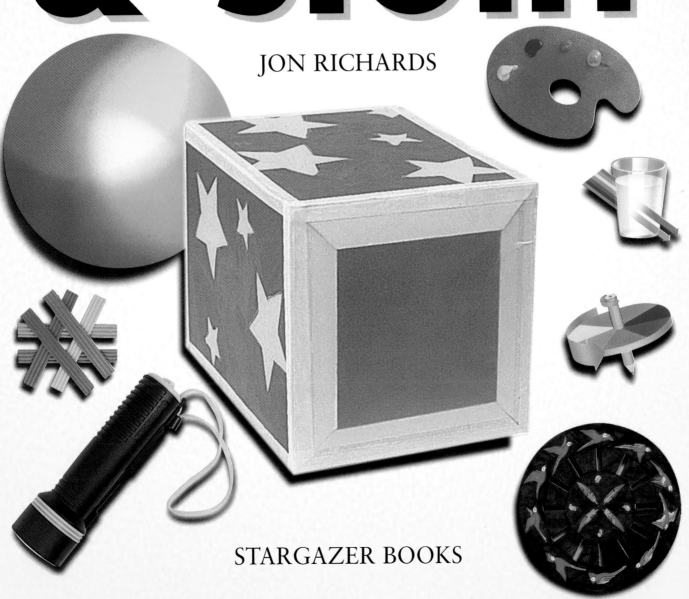

STARGAZER BOOKS

New edition published in 2005

Designed and produced by
Aladdin Books Ltd

First paperback edition published in
the United States in 2005 by
Stargazer Books
c/o The Creative Company
123 South Broad Street
P.O. Box 227
Mankato, Minnesota 56002

© Aladdin Books Ltd 1999

Design
David West
Children's Book Design

Designer
Flick Killerby

Illustrators
Ian Moores & Ian Thompson

Printed in U.A.E.

Cataloging-in-Publication data is
available from the Library of
Congress.

ISBN: 1-932799-66-4

ABOUT THE BOOK

Light and Sight examines the basic aspects of light, as well as its more complex and practical uses. By following the projects carefully, the readers are able to develop their practical skills, while at the same time expanding their scientific knowledge. Other ideas then offer them the chance to explore each aspect further to build up a more comprehensive understanding of the subject.

CONTENTS

YOUR FACTORY

BEFORE YOU START any of the projects, it is important that you learn a few simple rules about the care of your Science Factory.

● Always keep your hands and work surfaces clean. Dirt can damage results and ruin a project!

● Read all the instructions carefully before you start each project.

● Make sure you have all the equipment you need for the projects (see checklist opposite).

● If you don't have the right piece of equipment, then improvise. For example, a liquid detergent bottle will do just as well as a plastic drink bottle.

● Don't worry if you make mistakes. Just start again — patience is very important!

● Now you are ready to start. Turn the page and remember to have fun in your Science Factory!

Equipment checklist:
- ● Paper and cardboard
- ● Shallow trays
- ● Tissue, blotting, and tracing paper
- ● Scissors, adhesive tape, and glue
- ● Cotton balls and sprout seeds
- ● Paper fasteners and rubber bands
- ● Flashlights and rulers
- ● Cardboard boxes and tubes
- ● Modeling clay and beads
- ● Pencils, felt-tip pens, and paints
- ● Small mirrors and blankets
- ● Colored plastic wrap
- ● Plastic bottles and corks
- ● Eyepiece and convex lenses
- ● Drinking straws
- ● Large glass bowl
- ● Bulldog clips, pins, and nails
- ● Glass jar
- ● Milk

WARNING:
Some of the experiments in this book need the help of an adult. Always ask a grownup to give you a hand when you are using electrical appliances or sharp objects, such as scissors.

LIGHT FOR LIFE

WHAT YOU NEED
Shallow tray
Cotton balls
Sprout seeds
Cardboard

THE BRIGHTEST AND MOST OBVIOUS SOURCE OF LIGHT IS OUR NEAREST STAR, THE SUN. The sun supplies us, as well as plants and animals, with light and warmth — without it we would not be able to survive! This experiment offers an introduction to the world of light by showing you just how important sunlight is in keeping plants alive.

GROWING PLANTS

1 *Spread the cotton balls in the tray. Moisten the cotton balls with water and scatter the sprout seeds over them. Leave it until the seeds have sprouted.*

2 *Ask an adult to cut out your initials or a pattern from the cardboard. Place this over the seedlings.*

3 *Leave the tray in a sunny spot for about two weeks, keeping the cotton balls moist with water.*

4 *When the sprouts have fully grown, remove the cardboard. You will see that the sprouts exposed to the light by your cutout initials are much greener.*

TURNING SEEDS

Plants always grow toward the light. You can see this by placing a seedling on a windowsill. After one week you will see that it has started to grow toward the light. Turn the pot around, and it will start to grow back toward the light.

WHY IT WORKS

Plants use sunlight, a gas in the air called carbon dioxide, and water to make food that they use to grow. At the same time, they release a gas called oxygen into the air. If the plants are kept in the dark, they cannot make their food, so they will wither and be paler than those exposed to the sun.

SUNLIGHT

CARBON DIOXIDE ABSORBED

WATER ABSORBED

OXYGEN RELEASED

IN CAMERA

WHAT YOU NEED
*Cardboard box
Sharp pencil
Tracing paper
Paints
Adhesive tape
Blanket*

LIGHT FROM THE SUN, AS WELL AS ALL OTHER FORMS OF LIGHT, travels in straight lines as light rays. As a result, light cannot naturally turn corners (if you turn to pages 12-13, you will see how light can be made to go around objects). This creates events such as shadows (see pages 10-11). It can even appear to turn the world upside down, as this project to make your own pinhole camera reveals.

PINHOLE CAMERA

1 *Ask an adult to cut the back off a cardboard box. Decorate the box using the paints.*

2 *Ask an adult to make a small round hole in the front of the box using a sharp pencil.*

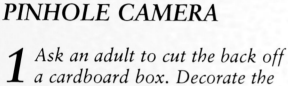

8

BLURRED IMAGE

Using the sharp pencil, ask an adult to make the hole in your camera slightly larger. The image on the screen will become fuzzy. This is because the larger hole lets more light rays enter the camera. These light rays then hit the screen at lots of different angles, making the picture become fuzzy.

3 Tape a sheet of tracing paper to the back of the box.

4 Pull the blanket over your head and the back of the camera. Point the camera at a bright window and you will be able to see an upside-down image of the window on the tracing paper in the back of the box.

WHY IT WORKS

The opening of the pinhole camera is very small. When rays of light from the window enter the camera, they cross over because they travel in a straight line. As a result, the image on the screen is upside down. The same thing happens with your eye. Light rays cross over as they pass through the pupil and enter the eyeball. When they hit the retina, they form an upside-down image. This image is sent to the brain, which turns the picture around again, letting you see the world the right way up!

OBJECT · LIGHT RAYS · PUPIL · RETINA · IMAGE

IN THE DARK

NOW THAT YOU KNOW THAT LIGHT RAYS TRAVEL IN STRAIGHT LINES (see pages 8-9), you can explore some of the effects of this. One of these effects is shadows. Look at your feet, and if it's a sunny day or you're in a bright room, you will see your shadow stretching off in the opposite direction from the light. This shadow is formed because your body blocks light rays and stops them from lighting up the dark area. Make your own puppet theater and have some fun experimenting with shadows.

WHAT YOU NEED
Dark cardboard
Paper fasteners
Tracing paper
Glue
Drinking straws
Flashlight

WHY IT WORKS

The dark area, or shadow, is caused by an absence of light. Rays of light from your flashlight are blocked by your puppet before they can reach the screen. This creates an area of the screen in the shape of your puppet that is darker than the rest of the screen. The completely dark part of the shadow is called the umbra.

UMBRA

SHADOW PUPPETS

1 Ask an adult to cut out the body parts of the puppets from the dark cardboard, as shown above.

2 Join the body parts together using the paper fasteners, making sure that the limbs can be moved.

3 Glue the straws to the feet of the puppet. These will help you to control the puppet.

4 Cut a semicircle out of a sheet of cardboard. Tape tracing paper over this hole to make the screen. Tape some cardboard supports to the back to keep the screen upright.

5 Shine the flashlight from behind the screen and entertain your friends by having your shadow puppets perform a story for them.

BLURRING SHADOWS

Move the puppets away from the screen, and their shadows become blurred, with an area of half-shadow around the edge. This half-shadow is called a penumbra.

11

BOUNCING LIGHT RAYS

THE PREVIOUS EXPERIMENTS HAVE SHOWN HOW LIGHT RAYS TRAVEL IN STRAIGHT LINES. However, with the right equipment, light rays can be made to go around corners! Shiny surfaces, such as mirrors, bounce light rays off them. This is called reflection. Use mirrors to build a periscope and see how you can make light turn corners.

WHAT YOU NEED
Cardboard
Ruler
Pencil
Two small mirrors
Adhesive tape

UP PERISCOPE

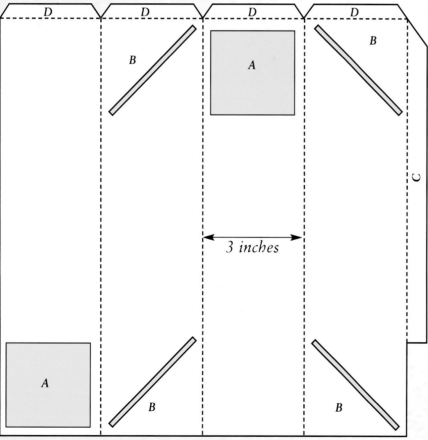

2 *Tape the edges of the mirrors. The mirrors should be slightly wider than your periscope.*

3 *Fold the periscope and tape it together to hold tab c in place. Tape some cardboard on top of the periscope using the four D tabs.*

1 *Using a ruler and pencil, draw an open plan of your periscope — like the one shown here — on the cardboard. Ask an adult to cut out the plan and two windows (A) and four slits to hold the mirrors (B).*

WHY IT WORKS

The shiny surfaces of the mirrors in your periscope reflect light rays. As a result, the rays of light that would normally travel over your head bounce off the mirrors, down through the periscope, and into your eye. This lets you see over any obstruction.

MIRROR

LIGHT FROM OBJECT

LIGHT REFLECTED OFF MIRROR INTO EYE

4 Slide the mirrors into the slots and use some adhesive tape to hold them in place. Now look through the lower mirror, and you will be able to use your periscope to see over tall objects such as a fence or a wall.

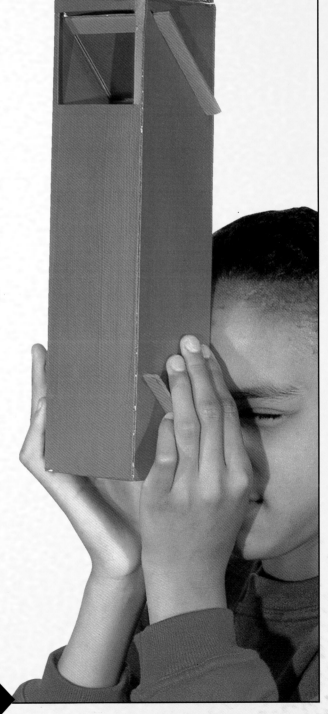

ODD REFLECTIONS

Look at your reflection on both sides of a metal spoon. Because the surfaces are curved, they will reflect light rays in different directions, giving you what looks like a funny-shaped face — one of the sides will even turn the image of your face upside down!

TRANSPARENT, TRANSLUCENT, AND OPAQUE

YOU'VE ALREADY SEEN HOW LIGHT IS BLOCKED BY SOME OBJECTS and reflected by others. Now you can see how light can actually pass through things! When light can pass through something, that object is called see-through, or transparent. However, some objects appear cloudy and only let some light through. They are called translucent. Other objects that let no light through are called opaque. This project will help you explore things that are transparent, translucent, and opaque.

WHAT YOU
NEED
Glass jar
Water
Milk
Flashlight

CLOUDY WATERS

1 *Fill the glass jar with water. Shine a flashlight through the water-filled jar onto a white screen behind it. You will see that white light from the flashlight travels all the way through the jar and the water.*

SEE-THROUGH PAPER

Hold a sheet of white paper up to the light, and it appears opaque. Now soak the paper in water, hold it up, and you will see that light can pass through it. This is because the water that soaks into the paper helps light pass through the gaps between the tiny paper fibers.

WHY IT WORKS

When you pour your milk into the water, the milk particles that float in the liquid scatter some of the colors that make up the white light (see the Splitting Light light (see the Splitting Light experiment on pages 20-21), leaving only orange and red to travel through. As a result, the liquid is translucent. When you add more milk, the particles block out the light completely, making the liquid opaque.

ORANGE AND RED LIGHT PASS THROUGH THE CLOUDY LIQUID

ALL THE SPECTRUM'S COLORS ENTER THE GLASS

2 *Pour a little milk into the the the water and stir it well to form a cloudy liquid. Shine the flashlight through the liquid again and this time you will see that the light on the screen is an orange color.*

3 *Add more milk to the water until the liquid turns completely white. Shine the flashlight on the glass once more, and you will see that no light is able to travel through the glass and the liquid, leaving just a shadow of the glass on the screen.*

15

BENDING LIGHT

THE EXPERIMENT ON PAGES 12-13 showed you how light can be reflected to turn corners, but it can also be helpful to bend light rays slightly. This bending is called refraction. Eyeglasses use refraction to bend rays of light, helping people to see things clearly. Microscopes also bend light rays to make objects appear bigger. Make a simple microscope in this project and see how bending light rays can be useful.

WHAT YOU
NEED

*Clear plastic
bottle
Small, flat
mirror
Modeling clay
Drop of water
Scissors*

MICROSCOPE

2 *Ask an adult to cut two horizontal slits in the other two sides of the bottle, near the top.*

1 *Ask an adult to cut the top off a plastic bottle and then cut out a narrow strip from two opposite sides of the lower half of the bottle.*

3 *Push the two ends of one of the plastic strips through these two slits to form a platform.*

BROKEN PENCILS

Fill a glass with water and place a pencil in it. When you look at the pencil from the side it appears as if the part of the pencil in the water has become bent or broken. This is because the water refracts, or bends, light rays from the pencil, making the underwater part appear as if it is in a slightly different position.

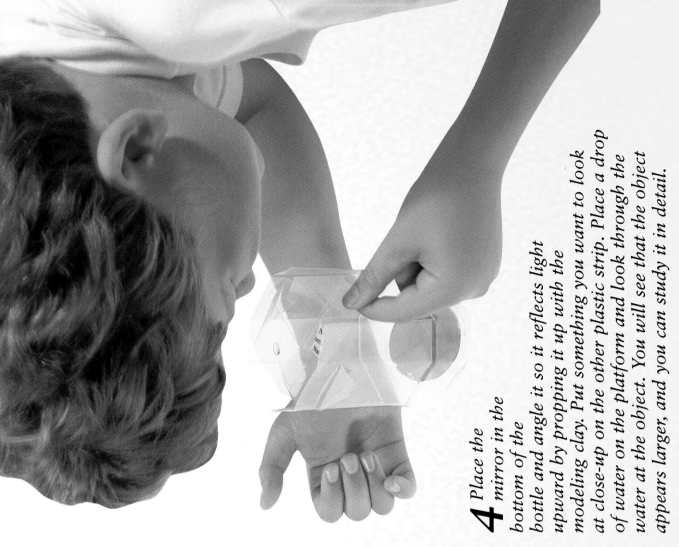

4 Place the mirror in the bottom of the bottle and angle it so it reflects light upward by propping it up with the modeling clay. Put something you want to look at close-up on the other plastic strip. Place a drop of water on the platform and look through the water at the object. You will see that the object appears larger, and you can study it in detail.

WHY IT WORKS

The drop of water on the platform acts as a small lens. When light rays from the object pass through the drop of water, they are bent, or refracted. This occurs in such a way that they make the object appear larger when you look at it.

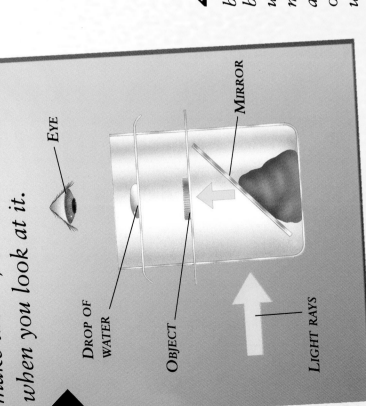

EYE

DROP OF WATER

OBJECT

MIRROR

LIGHT RAYS

17

BRINGING IT CLOSER

TELESCOPES HAVE BEEN USED FOR HUNDREDS OF YEARS to look at faraway objects. Just like the microscope you made on the previous page, many telescopes use bulging, or convex, lenses to bend, or refract, light rays. This makes objects appear closer than they actually are. Build your own telescope in this project and see how it can boost your power of vision.

LOOKING INTO THE DISTANCE

1 *Fit one of the convex lenses in one end of the wide cardboard tube.*

2 *Fit the other lens into the eyepiece.*

3 *Insert the eyepiece into one end of the narrow cardboard tube. Hold it in place using some of the modeling clay.*

WHY IT WORKS

The lens at the front of the telescope gathers light rays from far away, while the lens in the eyepiece bends these light rays again to produce a larger image. By sliding the tubes back and forth you can make objects at different distances come into focus.

LIGHT RAYS

18

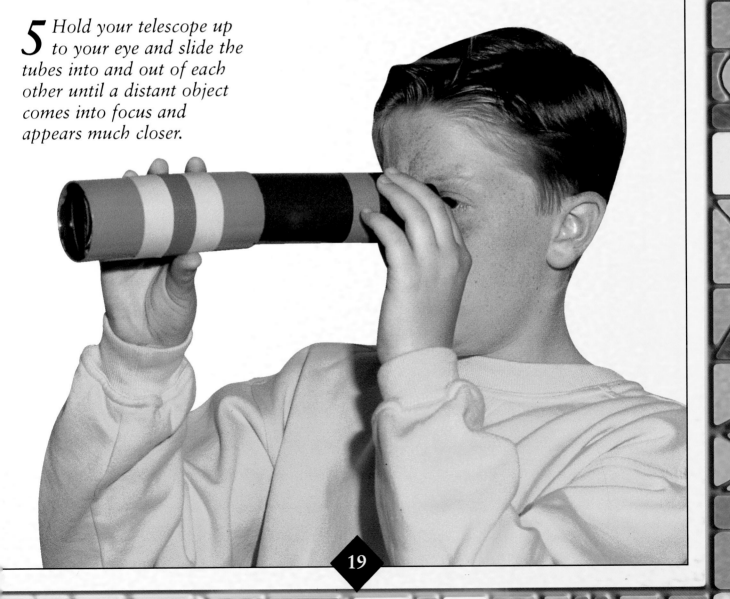

4 Push the narrow tube into the wide tube, making sure they slide together smoothly.

FOCUSING LIGHT

Hold one of the lenses in front of a flashlight and shine the light onto a wall. Now move the lens toward and away from the flashlight. You will see that the size of the light beam changes as you move the lens. You should be able to focus the light into a small dot on the wall.

5 Hold your telescope up to your eye and slide the tubes into and out of each other until a distant object comes into focus and appears much closer.

Splitting Light

In the experiment on pages 14-15, you learned that light can come in different colors. This is because what we see as white light is actually lots of different colors mixed together. Sometimes these colors split to form a rainbow. This multicolored band of light is called a spectrum. You can split white light up into a spectrum with this simple project.

SPLITTING WHITE LIGHT

1 Seal the edges of the mirror with the adhesive tape.

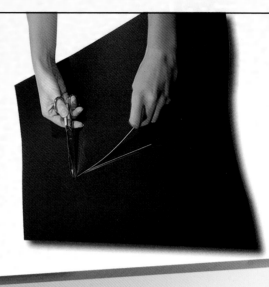

2 Ask an adult to cut a narrow slit in the middle of the black cardboard.

WHY IT WORKS

The angled mirror creates a triangular-shaped region near the surface of the water. This shape is called a prism. As sunlight travels through the prism, the light is split up to form a spectrum. Raindrops act as tiny prisms, splitting sunlight to create rainbows.

WHITE LIGHT HITS WATER

WHITE LIGHT SPLIT INTO A SPECTRUM BY THE WATER

3 Half-fill the glass bowl with water.

4 Using the bulldog clips, fix the mirror in the bowl of water so that it rests at an angle.

5 Point the mirror at a bright window and place the black cardboard in front of it. Now place the white cardboard below the slit and adjust the mirror until you see a spectrum appear on the piece of white cardboard.

COMPACT COLORS

Look at the playing surface of a compact disc. The tiny notches etched onto the surface split light up, creating a spectrum that you will be able to see as you view the compact disc from different angles.

MIXING LIGHT

WHAT YOU NEED
Three flashlights
Red, blue, and green plastic wrap
Three cardboard tubes
Adhesive tape
White cardboard

JUST AS YOU CAN SPLIT LIGHT INTO DIFFERENT COLORS (see pages 20-21), so you can mix colored lights together. Televisions use this principle to make color pictures. Look very closely at your television screen (not for too long, though!), and you will see that it is made up of thousands of tiny blue, red, and green dots. This project shows how you can mix colored lights to form new colors.

COLOR WHEELS

Color a circle of white cardboard with the colors of the spectrum in different segments. Ask an adult to push a sharp pencil through the middle. Then spin the wheel as fast as you can. The colors on the wheel will appear to blur and mix, making the wheel look white.

COLORED SPOTS

1 *Cut out squares of the red, blue, and green plastic wrap that are big enough to fit over the ends of the cardboard tubes.*

2 *Fix the plastic wrap to the ends of the tubes using the adhesive tape.*

WHY IT WORKS

The new colors are made by mixing the three colored lights on the white background. For example, red and green will form yellow. If you mixed all three colors together, they would form white light!

3 Place a sheet of white cardboard on the floor in a darkened room. With a couple of friends, hold the tubes and shine the flashlights down them onto the white cardboard.

4 Now move the spots of colored light so that they overlap and create new colors of light on the cardboard.

SEPARATING COLORS

Mixing colored lights (see pages 22-23) is not the only way to create new colors. Just like the colors on a television screen, the colors on this page are made up from tiny dots. This time the colors of these dots are magenta (pink), cyan (blue), yellow, and black. These colors, called pigments, are mixed together in different quantities to create all the other colors.

(SEE PAGES 22-23)

WHAT YOU NEED
Water-based felt-tip pens
Blotting paper
Bowl of water

SPLITTING PIGMENTS

1 *Cut the blotting paper into strips and draw patterns on them using a different colored marker for each strip.*

2 *Place the strips in the bowl so that only their bottoms are in the water while the rest hangs over the side.*

3 *Watch as the water soaks into the strips of blotting paper and starts to separate the ink into its different colored ingredients, or pigments.*

4 *When the water has completely soaked the strips of blotting paper, take them out and closely examine the strips to see which pigments make up each color.*

INKY RINGS

Cut out a circle of blotting paper. Draw a large spot in the middle, using a water-based marker. Then cut a strip from the spot in the center to the edge and fold it down so that it hangs in the water. As the water soaks into the paper, the color will separate, forming circles of pigments.

WHY IT WORKS

As the water soaks into the strips of blotting paper, it carries the pigments with it because they are water soluble (they can mix with water). However, the different pigments that make up the colors are carried by the water at different rates. As a result, the pigments are separated into bands, allowing you to see which pigments make up the colors. For example, red ink is made up of yellow and magenta pigments.

LIVING PICTURES

WHAT YOU
NEED
Cardboard
Colored pens
Nail
Bead
Cork
Mirror

ALL THROUGH THIS BOOK YOU HAVE SEEN the different aspects of light, from what light is made up of to how light rays can be altered to enlarge or color things. One other practical use for light is to create moving images, such as the ones you see when you go to the movies. This experiment will show you how moving pictures "move" and how this is all an illusion!

FLYING PARROT

2 Color the pictures using the colored pens. Ask an adult to cut out a series of slits around the middle of the circle using a sharp knife.

1 Ask an adult to cut out a large circle of cardboard. Then draw the images in the design shown on the opposite page.

3 Ask an adult to pierce the center of the cardboard circle with the nail. Slide the bead onto the nail and then push the cork on to make a handle.

FLIP BOOK

Draw each of the parrot illustrations on the corner of a pad of paper. Now flip through the pages very quickly using your thumb. Once again, the parrot appears to move.

You are not really seeing a moving parrot, but a series of slightly different pictures. When these pictures are seen very quickly, one after the other, they give the impression that the parrot is moving. Movie projectors work in the same way. They flash separate still images onto a screen very quickly, making it look like the picture is moving — when really it isn't!

4 Ask a friend to hold the mirror in front of you. Look through the slits from the back of your cardboard disk and spin it quickly. You will see that the parrot looks as if it is flying.

27

BEAMS OF LIGHT

As well as projecting moving pictures onto a movie screen (see pages 26-27), light can be used to carry lots of information along miles and miles of special glass wires called fiber-optic cables.

These beams of light can carry sound and pictures, such as telephone conversations and television pictures. This experiment shows you how these cables can carry light rays over the most winding routes, despite the fact that light travels in a straight line.

WHAT YOU NEED
Black paint
Flashlight
Pin
Large glass bowl
Clear plastic bottle

FIBER OPTICS

1 *Ask an adult to cut the top off the plastic bottle. Paint the outside of the bottle black, leaving a small area clear on one side. Using the pin, make a small hole in the bottle on the opposite side from the clear area.*

WHY IT WORKS

The stream of water acts like a fiber-optic wire. As the rays of light travel down the stream, they bounce, or reflect, off the sides, traveling along the stream even as it bends. The rays of light hit the stream's sides at such a shallow angle that they are reflected inside. In the same way, fiber-optic cables carry light rays along a curved path by reflecting them off the sides of the fibers.

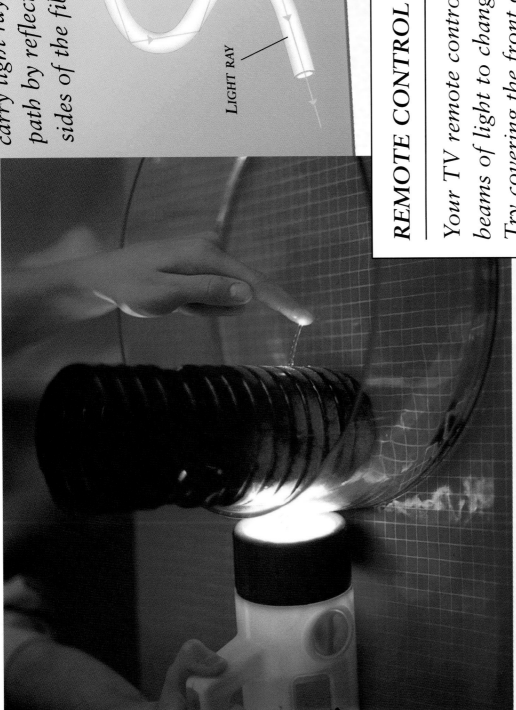

GLASS FIBER

LIGHT RAY

2 In a darkened room, stand the bottle against one side of the bowl so that the clear area faces out. Fill the bottle with water and shine the flashlight through the clear area. Place your finger in the stream of water and you should be able to see a spot of light.

FINDING OUT MORE

OPAQUE When no light can pass through an object, it is called opaque. *Find out how to make water opaque on pages 14-15, and see the effects of opaque objects with your shadow theater on pages 10-11.*

REFLECTION This occurs when light rays bounce off a shiny surface, such as a mirror. *Turn to pages 12-13 and see how reflection makes a periscope work. Can you find any other examples of reflection. Hint: look on pages 28-29.*

REFRACTION This occurs when light rays are bent as they travel through an object. *See refraction in action on pages 16-17 and 18-19 when you build a microscope and a telescope.*

EYE IN THE SKY

The Hubble Space Telescope actually orbits the earth. It is so powerful that it can see objects 14 billion light-years away!

NIGHT-LIGHT

Some animals can make their own light. This is called bioluminescence. Fireflies and glowworms flash lights in their abdomens to attract a mate.

SHADOW A dark area caused by an object blocking out light rays. *Build your own shadow theater on pages 10-11.*

ON DISPLAY

Many animals use color to display. Birds of Paradise, which live in rainforests of the Pacific, have bright feathers.

SPECTRUM

Using a specially shaped piece of glass called a prism, sunlight can be split up into a band of colors. This band is called a spectrum. *You can see a spectrum on pages 20-21.*

TRANSLUCENT

When only some light rays are able to pass through an object, it is called translucent. *See how you can make water translucent by adding a small amount of milk on pages 14-15.*

TRANSPARENT

Objects are transparent when they let light pass through them freely. As a result, you can see through them completely. *Take a look through the book and find some transparent objects. Then see if you can find any more transparent objects around your home.*

LARGE STARS

The night sky is full of stars of different colors, such as red, yellow, and blue. Some of these stars are enormous — over 600 times bigger than our sun!

VEGA

ALDEBARAN

THE SUN

BETELGEUSE

INDEX